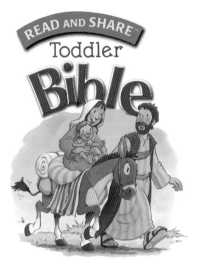

READ AND SHARE™
Toddler
Bible

For:

_____

From:

_____

Date:

_____

Read and Share™ Toddler Bible

© 2009 by Thomas Nelson, Inc.

Stories retold by Gwen Ellis

Illustrations by Steve Smallman

Published in Nashville, Tennessee, by Thomas Nelson. Thomas Nelson is a registered trademark of Thomas Nelson, Inc.

Scripture quotations are taken from INTERNATIONAL CHILDREN'S BIBLE®. © 1986, 1988, 1999 by Thomas Nelson, Inc. Used by permission.

Thomas Nelson, Inc., titles may be purchased in bulk for educational, business, fund-raising, or sales promotional use. For information, please e-mail SpecialMarkets@ThomasNelson.com.

Library of Congress Cataloging-in-Publication Data

Ellis, Gwen.
    Read and share toddler Bible / stories retold by Gwen Ellis ; illustrations
        by Steve Smallman.
        p. cm.
    Includes bibliographical references and index.
    ISBN 978-1-4003-1464-5 (hardcover : alk. paper) 1. Bible stories, English.
        I. Smallman, Steve. II. Title.
    BS551.3.E552 2009
    220.9'505—dc22

                                                    2009004642

Printed in China

09 10 11 12 13 RRD 5 4 3 2 1

READ AND SHARE™
Toddler
Bible

Stories retold by Gwen Ellis

Illustrations by Steve Smallman

THOMAS NELSON
Since 1798

NASHVILLE   DALLAS   MEXICO CITY   RIO DE JANEIRO   BEIJING

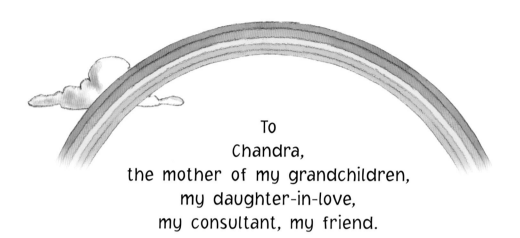

To
Chandra,
the mother of my grandchildren,
my daughter-in-love,
my consultant, my friend.

And to
the children of New Hope Centre,
Bethany, Swaziland.

A Word to Parents:

If you are the parent of a toddler, congratulations! These little ones are charming, busy, exhausting, and curious little sponges ready to soak up God's Word.

The *Read and Share Toddler Bible* has been written and designed specifically for these precious little ones. The simplified, yet biblically sound stories are filled with exciting action words, such as *whoosh* and *clippety-clop*, that your little one will love to hear again and again. Simple, charming art invites your toddler to study the pictures as you read the stories. To further reinforce the concepts, suggestions for interactive learning accompany each story—such as to act out the story or to make a simple craft. Be sure to include these activities as they will not only help your child learn God's Word, but they will also provide parent and child together time.

Above all, enjoy this special time with your toddler, a time when life is all about learning. Help your little one learn about the love of God—that God is always with us, loving and caring for us, and that we can always pray for His help. And remember: What is true for your child, is true for you as well. God loves you, and He will give you the wisdom, patience, and love you need to be a great parent.

Blessings on you and yours,
Gwen Ellis

Contents

Old Testament Stories

New Testament Stories

Shout to the Lord, all the earth.
Serve the Lord with joy.
Come before him with singing.
Know that the Lord is God.
He made us, and we belong to him.

—Psalm 100:1-3

Old Testament

In the Beginning

God made everything.
He made the warm sun to light up the day.

He made the moon
   to light up the night.
He made all the pretty stars too.

God made puffy clouds and flowers and trees.

God made wiggly fishes. *Splish! Splash!*

God made big birds and little birds. *Flap! Flap!*

God made all the animals—
 puppies, kitties, bears, and many, many more.
God made man. "Hello, Adam."
Then God made woman. "Hello, Eve."
God was happy!

PARENTS: Help your little one use pictures of animals and flowers from old magazines to make a collage. Together name each of the animals and flowers, and then thank God for making them.

Adam and Eve and the Sneaky Snake

Adam and Eve were God's friends.
They lived in a beautiful garden.
Sometimes God came to visit them.

There were many wonderful things to eat
  in the garden.
But God said, "See that tree? Don't eat its
  fruit. You must stay away from it."

One day a s-s-s-sneaky s-s-s-snake
came s-s-s-slithering up to Eve.
"Hello, Eve, have you ta-s-s-s-sted
this-s-s-s fruit?"

"Oh no!" Eve said. "God said it was a no-no."
"Try it," whi-s-s-s-spered the snake.
    "It won't hurt you."
  So Eve ate a fruit. She gave Adam a bite.
    Mmmm, good!

Uh-oh! Something happened.
Adam and Eve felt so bad that they hid.
They knew they had made a wrong choice.

God came to visit.
"Adam, Eve, where are you?
    Why are you hiding? Did you eat
    fruit from the tree?" God asked.
"Yes," they said.
 God was very sad.
"Out you go," God said. "You can't live
    in the garden anymore."

PARENTS: Talk with your child about what is a
"no-no" at your house. Ask her what will happen
if she disobeys and does a no-no. Reassure her that
Mommy, Daddy, and God will still love her even if
she makes a wrong choice.

Out of
the Garden

Outside the garden, Adam and Eve had to
   work hard to grow their food.
They planted vegetable seeds.
Guess what came up. Vegetables—*and weeds!*

Adam and Eve had made a wrong choice.
But God still loved them,
    and He was always with them.
When we make wrong choices,
    God still loves us, and He is always
    with us.

PARENTS: Little children need to know that
even when they have made a wrong choice,
Mommy and Daddy still love them, and God
still loves them too. Pray with your child to
ask forgiveness for a wrong choice.

Noah and the Big Boat

"Noah," God called, "I want you to build
a big boat."
"Okay," Noah said, "I'll do it right away."
And Noah went to get his tools.

Noah picked up his hammer and some nails.
He found some boards and his saw.
Then Noah went to work.
Pound! Pound! Saw! Saw!

When the boat was finished, Noah, Mrs. Noah,
and their three sons and their wives all
went up the ramp and into the boat.
"Bring two of every kind of animal inside,"
said God.

Soon the animals came two by two into the boat:
two elephants, two kangaroos, two pandas,
two pigs, two bunnies—two of every animal.
"Come on in," called Noah.

Noah led the elephants into their stall.
Mrs. Noah found a place for the kitties to sleep.
Noah's sons helped all the other animals
    find a place to rest.

Crrrrrreak! Crrrrrreak! God shut the door
   of the boat.
It started to rain. *Pitter-patter. Pitter-patter.*
The wind blew. *Oooo! Ooooo!*
Inside the boat, everyone was snug and safe.

PARENTS: Let your little one pretend to pound and
saw like Noah. Let him be one of the animals climbing
up the ramp. He can pitter-patter like the rain and
howl like the wind. Then help your child thank God
for keeping him safe.

29

In and Out
of the Boat

It rained and rained and rained some more,
    but everyone in the boat was dry.
The kitties purred.
The bunnies hopped.
The puppies chased their tails.

Mr. and Mrs. Noah were busy.
Every day they gave the animals food.
And they gave the animals water too.
They took good care of all the animals.

After floating on the water for a long time,
Noah let a white dove fly out the window.

The dove brought back a green leaf.
The trees were growing!
Noah let the dove out again.
    It didn't come back.
The water was gone!

"Time to come out of the boat," said Noah.
Lickety-split, everyone hurried out.
They ran and hopped for joy.
God smiled and put a rainbow in the sky.
He promised never to flood the earth again.

PARENTS: Cut strips of paper of different colors. Help your little one glue the strips on a large sheet of paper to make a rainbow. Talk to your child about how the rainbow stands for God's promise.

35

Genesis
12:1–7; 17:1–16;
22:17

Abram and the New Land

God told Abram to go on a trip.
Abram didn't know where he was going.
He didn't have a map.
As he walked, God showed him the way.

Abram's wife Sarai, his nephew,
  his servants, and all his animals
  went on the trip too.
They all walked and walked until
  Abram saw a beautiful place.
"You can keep this home forever," God said.

Abram and Sarai were happy to be home.
All the servants and animals were happy
  to be home too.
God changed Abram's name to Abraham.
He changed Sarai's name to Sarah.

Then God made them a promise.
"Your children and grandchildren will
be as many as the stars."

PARENTS: Pretend with your little one to be Abram and
Sarai going on a long walk. Your child must trust you to
lead her from room to room. At the end of your "trip"
have a treat for her. Explain that we can trust God to
lead us every day of our life—and that He will!

A Baby for
Abraham and Sarah

Abraham and Sarah wanted a baby very much.
They waited and waited, but no baby came.
Then they were too old.

One day three visitors came to Abraham's tent.
"Please stay for lunch," said Abraham.
Abraham said to Sarah, "Please bake some bread."
Then Abraham hurried to get some meat to cook.

When the yummy food was ready,
the three men sat down to eat.
"God promises that Sarah will have a baby
next year," one of the men said.

Sarah laughed.
"I'm too old to have a baby," she said.
But nothing is too hard for God!

The next year, Sarah did have a baby boy.
Sarah was so happy she laughed again.
Sarah named her baby Isaac.
Isaac means "laughing."

God promised Abraham a son,
    and God always keeps His promises.
God has many promises for you too,
    and God will keep His promises to you.

PARENTS: Keeping promises is very important to
little ones. Make a simple promise to your child,
such as reading a favorite story at bedtime. Keep
your promise, and then remind him that God
always keeps His promises.

Rebekah and the Ten Camels

Isaac was all grown up.
It was time for him to have a wife.
Isaac's daddy, Abraham, decided to
find a wife for him.

Abraham said to his best servant,
    "Please find a wife for Isaac."
His servant loaded up ten camels
    with presents.
Then he went far away across the desert.

The servant stopped beside a well.
"Dear God, show me the best girl for Isaac.
If she gives me *and* my camels water,
I'll know she's the right one."
Soon a girl named Rebekah came.
"Please give me water," Abraham's servant said.

"Yes, I will give you and your ten camels water," said Rebekah.

This was the right girl for Isaac.

Jacob and Esau

Isaac and Rebekah had two boys.
The boys were twins.
One was red and hairy. His name was Esau.
The other, named Jacob, had smooth skin.

Esau liked to hunt and fish.
Jacob liked to stay home and cook.
One day Esau was hungry.
Jacob had a big pot of soup.

"Give me some soup," said Esau.

"Okay," said Jacob, "but first give me all the gifts
    Dad has for you."

"Sure, just give me some soup," said Esau.

Jacob got Esau's gifts.
Then Jacob tricked their father, Isaac, and
    got even more of Esau's gifts.
Esau was so angry, he wanted to hurt Jacob.
Jacob ran far away across the desert.

Jacob
IS Tricked

Jacob ran far away to his uncle's house,
where he met Rachel. She was beautiful.
Jacob loved Rachel, and Rachel loved Jacob.

Jacob and Rachel wanted to get married.
But then someone tricked Jacob.
Oh, they tricked him good!

On their wedding day, the bride wore a heavy
    scarf over her face.
Jacob couldn't see through the scarf.
When the scarf came off—*surprise!*
It wasn't Rachel. It was her sister, Leah.
Jacob was angry. He didn't like this trick.
Some tricks are funny, but some are not.

PARENTS: The lesson of this story is that we eventually get what we give. Talk with your little one about how to be kind to others. Let him know God is happy when he is kind.

JOSEPH AND HIS BROTHERS

Jacob had lots of sons.
He had more sons than you have fingers.
Jacob loved all his sons,
   but he loved Joseph the most.
That made the other brothers angry.
When Joseph came to see them,
   they had scowls on their faces.

Joseph told them, "I had a dream. In my
    dream your wheat all bowed down to mine."
The brothers scowled even more.
They thought Joseph wanted to be their king!

"Do you think you will rule over us?
You will not be the king of us!" the angry
brothers screamed.
They were angrier than ever with Joseph.

PARENTS: Tell your little one that Jacob had 12 sons in all.
Hold up her 10 fingers, along with 2 of your own, to show 12.
Show her what a *scowl* is. Then talk with her about being
kind to others—especially to brothers and sisters.

Joseph and His Beautiful Coat

Jacob gave Joseph a beautiful coat.
It was blue, red, green, and yellow.
Joseph was proud of his coat.
He wore it everywhere.

"Joseph, go see your brothers," Jacob said.
"I'll wear my new coat," said Joseph.
When the brothers saw Joseph coming,
    they were *sooooo* angry.

"I don't like him," one brother said.
"Let's get rid of him," another said.
They grabbed Joseph.
They threw him down a hole. Poor Joseph.

Some men on camels came riding by.
They were going to Egypt.
"Would you like to buy a boy?" the brothers asked.
"Sure," the men said.
So the brothers sold Joseph.
Away he went to Egypt.

In Egypt, a rich man took Joseph home.
Joseph had to work hard for him.
Joseph did a very good job.

But one day, the man's wife
told a lie about Joseph.
The rich man threw Joseph in
jail. Poor Joseph.

PARENTS: Draw happy, sad, angry, and scared faces on a piece
of paper. Read the story again and ask your little one to identify
the emotions Joseph and his brothers were feeling. Explain
that God understands how we feel, and He will help us.

JOSEPH HELPS a King

Now Joseph lived in jail.
It was *not* fun.
A man in jail told Joseph his dream.
God showed Joseph what the man's dream meant.

Joseph told the man that he would get out of jail.
"You are going to work for the king," Joseph said.
And that's what happened.
"Tell the king about me," said Joseph.
But the man forgot all about Joseph.

Then, one night, the king had a scary, bad
  dream.
The man from the jail remembered Joseph.
The man told the king, "Joseph can tell you
  what your dream means."

The king said, "Get Joseph out of jail.
Bring him here right now."

Joseph came to the king's house.
God showed Joseph all about the king's dream.
Joseph said, "Get ready. A hungry time
 is coming."
The king said, "Will you help us find enough food?"
"Yes," Joseph said.
"You are now a ruler," said the king.

As a ruler, Joseph had much food
stored for the hungry times.

One day Joseph's hungry brothers
came looking for food.

They didn't recognize Joseph.
Joseph was not mean to them.
He was kind.
"I am your brother," he said.
Everyone was happy.

PARENTS: Help your little one understand that God can make even bad things turn out to be good things— because He loves us.

Baby Moses

Baby Moses was a wee tiny baby.
When he cried, his mother rocked him.
Back and forth and back and forth.
Baby Moses went to sleep.

A bad king wanted to hurt Baby Moses.
So his mother hid him.
Baby Moses got bigger.
Soon he was too big to hide.

His mother made a little basket.
She made the outside so the water
   couldn't get in.
She put a soft blanket inside.
She put Baby Moses in the basket.

Baby Moses' mother carried the basket to the river.
Gently, gently, she put the basket on the water.
Rock, rock, back and forth went the basket.
Baby Moses was safe inside the basket.

PARENTS: Let your little one act out this story. Remind him that God is watching over him.

The Good Sister

Baby Moses' mother went home.
But big sister Miriam stayed to watch Baby Moses.
She saw the princess pick up his basket.
The princess smiled at Baby Moses.

"I know someone who can help you with the baby," said Miriam.

"Oh, please get someone," said the princess.

Miriam ran home to get her mother.

Moses' mother got to take Baby Moses home for a long time.

PARENTS: Act out this story using a doll and a small basket. Remind your child that God is always watching over her because He loves her.

Moses
Leads the People

"Moses," God said, "lead My people to the
land I promised them."
Soon all God's people started walking to
their new home.
In the daytime,
they followed
a big cloud.

At night, a big fire in the sky helped
the people see.

One day the people came to the Red Sea.
"We're stuck," they said.
Moses held up his hand. *Whoosh!*
God made a path right through the water.

The people walked right across that sea.
Then they walked through the desert.
They walked beside a river.
They walked right to their Promised Land.

PARENTS: This is a story about trust. Hide a treat—
something your child likes—in one of your hands and
let him choose which hand. As he is choosing, say, "It's
something good, trust me."

The Donkey That Talked

Balaam's donkey went *clop-clopping* down the road.
Suddenly the donkey stopped.
Balaam almost fell off.
The donkey saw something in the road, but Balaam didn't see anything.

Balaam hit the donkey to make him go.
God made the donkey talk.
"Why are you hitting me?" asked the
    donkey.
"I want you to get going," Balaam said.

Then God helped Balaam see a bright,
shiny angel standing in the road.
"Why are you hitting your donkey?" asked
the angel.

"Your donkey knows more than you do,"
said the angel. "Now, go and help
God's people!"
So Balaam went to help God's people.
His donkey was very happy about that.

PARENTS: Make a donkey face by using a paper
plate. Glue on long ears and draw on a face. Let
your little one pretend to be the donkey.

Joshua and the Wall

Joshua loved God with all his heart.
He was a brave man.
It was his job to lead God's people
across the Jordan River and into the
Promised Land.

God made a dry path for them.
Thump, thump, thump went their sandals in
the sand.
They *thump, thumped* right up to a big city.

"Look," said one man. "Walls . . . big walls!
    How are we going to get in?"
God told Joshua what to do.

God said, "March around the city—
    one, two, three, four, five, six, seven days.
    March around seven times on the last day."

Around the city went Joshua.
Around the city went all the people.

"Why are we doing this?" the people asked.
"Keep marching," Joshua said.
The people marched around the wall for seven days.
On the last day, they marched around the wall seven times.

Kaboom!
God made the wall fall down.
Hooray for our God!

PARENTS: Act out the story by stacking up
pillows and marching around them. Let your
child help knock down the pillows.

David and the Sheep

David was a shepherd.
He took care of the sheep.
"Baa, baa," said the sheep.
They stood close to David.
When the sheep ran away,
 David brought them back.
When they got hurt,
 David fixed their owies.

David liked to play his harp.
The sheep liked to listen.
David made up songs.
He sang them to the sheep.

Out in the fields, David talked to God.
David sang songs to God.
God helped David take care of the sheep.
David loved God.

PARENTS: Make sheep by gluing cotton balls on an oval-shaped piece of paper. Add pipe cleaner legs, or just glue on paper legs. Let your little one sing to the sheep. Then help your child pray or sing to God.

David, the Youngest Boy

"Time to pick a new king," God said.
"Samuel, go to Bethlehem. I'll show you
who the new king will be."
Off to Bethlehem Samuel went.

He went to a man named Jesse.
"Hello," said Samuel. "I've come to pick
a new king. It will be one of your
sons. Ask all of them to come see me."

In came seven sons.
They were tall and handsome.
"It's none of them," said God.
"Do you have another son?" asked Samuel.
"Yes," said the father.
"Bring him here," said Samuel.
In came David.
He was the one God wanted to be king.

PARENTS: Play a game by asking your little one: Who does God love? Does He love the prettiest? Does He love the biggest? Does He love the littlest one? Of course, the answer to all the questions is "yes." End with: Does God love you? *Yes!*

David and the Giant

Goliath was a mean man.
He wanted to hurt God's people.
The soldiers were scared.
Goliath was much bigger than any of them.
Goliath was a big bully.

Goliath liked to scare people.
He yelled. He shook his fists.
He made mean faces.
Little David was not scared of him.
David knew God was on his side.

David picked up one, two, three,
    four, five stones.
He put one stone in his slingshot.
"God, please help me," he prayed.
Whirr! Whirr! went the slingshot.
Away flew the stone.
Down went the giant.
God helped David win the battle!

PARENTS: Explain to your little one that God can help us when we face difficult situations. Read the story again, and act out the motions described. Dance around the room with your child singing, "David won! God won! We win!"

The Birds Feed Elijah

Elijah was one of God's people.
But there was a bad king who did not like Elijah.
God told Elijah, "Hurry! Run away and hide!
Go out to a stream in the desert."

Elijah went to the little stream.
"Mmmm, good water to drink," Elijah said.
Growl! went Elijah's tummy.
"But what will I eat?" asked Elijah.

Flap, flap! A big bird was coming.
What did it have in its mouth?
A loaf of soft bread for Elijah's
   hungry tummy.
Yum! Yum!

Flap, flap! Another big bird came flying.
What did it have in its mouth?
A piece of juicy meat to eat.
God took good care of Elijah.

PARENTS: Let your little one pretend to be a bird and bring you bits of food. Or perhaps she'd rather be Elijah and have you bring her food. Say, "Thank you, bird. Thank You, God."

ELisHa HeLPS PeOPLe

Elisha was God's helper.
He liked to help people.
When some people were very hungry,
    Elisha gave them food.
The people were very happy.

Another time some men ate
   poisonous food.
Oooo! Their tummies hurt.
Elisha put some flour in their soup.
The men ate the soup.
They felt better.

A lady had a little boy.
She loved him very much.
But the boy got sick and died.

The lady hurried to get Elisha.
Elisha came. Elisha prayed.
"Achooo!" The boy sneezed.
He opened his eyes.
He was alive, and he
    was just fine.

PARENTS: Talk with your little one about how God uses people to help Him. Name some ways your child can help you. Tell him God is pleased when we help one another.

A Baby Prince

A baby who will be king is called a prince.
Most princes live in big castles.
But the baby prince
    Joash lived in
    God's house.
His nurse hid him
    there to keep
    him safe.

When Joash was seven years old,
some soldiers came and showed
him to all the people.
The people cheered for him to be
their new king.
Joash was king for a long time, and
the people were happy.

PARENTS: With your
child, make a paper
crown to wear while you
read this story. Tell your
little one that he or she is
a prince or princess in
God's kingdom.

Daniel in the Lions' Den

Daniel prayed to God in heaven three
   times every day.
But some mean men didn't like Daniel.
They had the king make a new law.
It said everyone must pray only to the king.
No, no, Daniel thought. *I must pray to God.*
   I can't pray to the king.

So Daniel went right on praying to God:
    one, two, three times a day.
The mean men saw him praying.
"Off to the king with you," they said.
The king could not break his own law.
"Daniel must go to the lions' den," he said sadly.

Daniel wasn't afraid. God would help him.
Roar! went the lions.
But they didn't bite Daniel.
God sent an angel to close the lions'
    mouths.

The next morning the king called,
        "Daniel, come out."
Daniel did. He was just fine.
Thank You, God!

PARENTS: Talk about how important it is to pray to
God. Make a picture prayer book by gluing pictures of
family and friends onto a folded paper booklet. Help
your child pray for each person in the book.

Thanks be to God for his gift that
is too wonderful to explain.

—2 Corinthians 9:15

New Testament

Mary and the Angel

Mary lived in Nazareth.
Soon she would marry Joseph.
Joseph was a carpenter.
He lived in Nazareth too.

One day Mary was busy working.
All at once, there was a bright
   light—the brightest light ever!
What was it?
It was a bright, shining angel.

Mary was scared.
"Don't be afraid," said the angel.
"God sent me."

"God is happy with you, Mary.
    You are going to have a baby boy.
    Name Him Jesus."

PARENTS: This is the best news ever! Jesus is God's Son. Put on some Christmas music, such as "Joy to the World!" and let your little one beat out the rhythm with a spoon and a pan.

JOSEPH MARRIES MARY

Pound! Pound! Saw! Saw!
Joseph made a table.
Pound! Pound! Saw! Saw!
Joseph fixed a door.
Joseph was a carpenter.
He made things with wood.

Joseph loved Mary.
Mary loved Joseph.
When Joseph heard Mary was
    going to have a baby, he
    was confused.

131

One night when Joseph went to
    sleep, he had a dream.
An angel talked to Joseph in his
    dream.

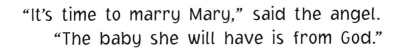

"It's time to marry Mary," said the angel.
"The baby she will have is from God."

Soon Joseph and Mary were married.
One day they had to go to another town
   far away.
It was the king's law.

So off they went.

Clippety-clop, clippety-clop.

Mary was so tired.

But where could she sleep?

There was no room for them at
the inn.

Joseph found a place for them
in a stable.

Kind Joseph made a soft bed
of hay for Mary.

PARENTS: Joseph was a kind man. Talk with your
little one about kindness. Ask her how she can be kind
to her pets. Her brothers and/or sisters. Her friends.

GOD'S
Baby Boy

Tiptoe, tiptoe into the stable.
Tiptoe past the cow.
Tiptoe past the donkey
   and the sheep.
Tiptoe up to Mary and Joseph.

Peek in the box; peek in and see.
It's a baby sleeping on the hay.
It's Baby Jesus.
It's God's Little Boy.

PARENTS: Put a baby doll in a box. Then let your little one act out tiptoeing to the manger to see the Baby Jesus.

Sleepy, Sleepy Shepherds

The stars are shining brightly.
It's very quiet and dark tonight.
Shhhh! Shhhh! The sheep are sleeping.
Shepherds are watching to keep them safe.

Oh my! What is that bright light?
It's an angel in the sky.
"Good news," the angel said. "Find
the baby in the hay.
He will be your Savior."

Off to Bethlehem town they ran
to look for the baby in the stable.
Tiptoe, tiptoe to the hay.
Oh what joy! What a happy day!

There in the straw is a tiny, wee one.
It is the Savior.
It is God's Baby Son.

PARENTS: Sing "Away in a
Manger" with your little one.

Presents for the Baby

Knock, knock. Someone is at the door.
"Who's there?" asks Mary.
"Wise men from far away," someone says.
Mary opens the door for the visitors.

"We have presents for the baby.
Would you like to see them?"
"Yes, thank you," said Mary and Joseph.
"Here are gold and good-smelling perfumes.
Gifts for a King," said the visitors.

PARENTS: Show your little one some shiny gold jewelry, and let him smell some perfume.

WHERE IS JESUS?

When Jesus was a little boy, He had to obey His mommy and daddy, just as you do.
He also had to obey His Father in heaven.

When Jesus was twelve years old,
   Mary and Joseph took Him on a trip.
They went to a big city called Jerusalem.
They went to God's Temple.

When it was time to go home,
  Mary and Joseph began walking.
They thought Jesus was with friends.
But He wasn't.

Where was Jesus?
They asked their friends, "Have you seen Jesus?"
No one had seen Him.
Mary and Joseph hurried back to Jerusalem.
They had to find their son.

They looked high. They looked low.
They finally found Jesus in the Temple.
He was talking to some teachers.
He knew the answers to all their questions.

"Jesus," Mary said, "we've been looking for You. We were worried about You."

"I was here in My Father's house," said Jesus. "I'll go home with you now."

PARENTS: Make a chart of simple tasks, such as picking up toys or taking a nap. Reward your little one with stickers and treats for completed tasks. This will help her learn obedience.

Jesus Heals a Little Boy

Jesus loves children.
When He lived on earth,
    He always had time for them.
He talked to them.
He prayed for them.

When a little boy got sick,
    his daddy went to find Jesus.
"Please come heal my little boy,"
    the daddy said.

"Go home," said Jesus. "Your little
    boy is well."
The daddy rushed home.
His servants ran out to meet him.
"Your little boy is all better. Come see!"
The daddy went inside his house.

There was his little boy,
all better and happy.
Thank You, Jesus!

PARENTS: Sing the song "Jesus Loves Me" with your
little one. Sing again, changing the first three words
to "Jesus sees me" or "Jesus heals me" or "Jesus hears
me" to emphasize Jesus' love for your child.

Jesus Helps a Little Girl

Many people came to Jesus for help.
One day another daddy came to Jesus.
"My little girl is very sick," he said.
"Will You help her?"

"Yes, I will come," said Jesus.
And Jesus started walking to the daddy's
    house.
But before He got there, the little girl died.
Oh, the daddy was so sad.

Jesus wasn't worried. He kept walking.
He went into the girl's room.
He took her by the hand and said,
   "Stand up!"
She stood up! She was all better.

PARENTS: Pray with your little one for someone
who is sick. Show a picture of the person, if
possible. Explain that Jesus hears us when we pray.

A Little Boy with a Lunch

Big crowds of people followed Jesus.
They listened to Him when He talked.
Sometimes they forgot to bring their lunch.
When that happened, they got very hungry.

"The people are hungry," said Jesus' friends.
"Give them food," said Jesus.
"We only have this little boy's lunch," they said.
"Please, little boy, may we have your lunch?"

The little boy gave his lunch to Jesus.
There were two little fish and
    five little loaves of bread.
Jesus prayed and thanked God for the food.

There were many, many, many
people there.
Jesus' friends gave fish and bread
to all the people.
Everyone had enough to eat.
They even had 12 baskets of bread
left over.

PARENTS: Share fish sticks with your little one
as you tell this story. Pray over the food before
you eat, and also give thanks after you finish.

Jesus Meets a Little Man

There was a small, little man
with a long, long name.
His long, long name was Zacchaeus.
More than anything, he wanted to see Jesus.

Walk, walk. Jesus came walking to
    Zacchaeus' town.
All the people came out to see Jesus.
Zacchaeus was very short.
Everyone was taller than Zacchaeus.
He couldn't see Jesus.

"I know," said Zacchaeus. "I'll climb up a tree.
    Then I can see Jesus."
  Walk, walk. Here comes Jesus.
"I see Him!" Zacchaeus was excited.

Stop, stop. Jesus stopped walking.
"Zacchaeus, come down here,"
    said Jesus.
"I want to go to your house."
Down came Zacchaeus.
He and Jesus walked home.

PARENTS: Encourage your
child to act out the opposites in
this story: up/down, short/tall,
walk/stop. For example, stoop
down low for "short" and stand
up on tiptoes for "tall."

One Lost Sheep

There once was a man who had
   100 sheep.
In the morning, he took them to the
   fields to eat.
At night, he brought them home
   to be safe.

Every night he counted them.
He counted them: one, two, three.
He counted all the way to . . . *99?*

One of his sheep was missing!
Where could it be?
"I have to go find my sheep,"
said the shepherd, and off he went.

The shepherd looked everywhere.
He looked in the low places.
He looked in the high places.
He looked behind rocks.
He looked under bushes.

Finally, he heard something.
"Baa, baa," said the lost sheep.
The shepherd hurried to find his sheep.
"It's okay," said the shepherd. "I've got
you now."

The shepherd lifted the sheep onto his
shoulders.
They went home as fast as they could.
"Baa, baa," said the other sheep.
They were happy that the lost sheep
was home.

PARENTS: Draw a picture of hills and trees. Give your little one
lots of cotton balls to glue on the page to make sheep. Don't glue
down one cotton ball, but move it back to the rest of the sheep as
you tell the story.

Luke 19:28–38;
John 12:12–16

Jesus and the Donkey

Jesus said to His friends, "Please go into town.
Find a young donkey.
Tell people the Master needs it.
Untie it and bring it to Me."

The friends wondered why Jesus wanted a donkey.
But they went to town, found the donkey, and brought it back to Jesus.

Jesus climbed on the donkey.
Down the street He went.
Clippety-clop went the donkey's feet.
"Look, Jesus is coming!" said the people.

The people cut branches from palm trees.
"Hooray! Praise God!" they shouted.
They remembered that God's Word said,
   "Your king will come, riding on a donkey."

Jesus had something important to do.
He had to die on a cross.
He died so that when we do wrong,
    we can be forgiven.

PARENTS: Make two hearts and a cross from white paper. Let your toddler color one heart black while you talk with him about the sins that make our hearts black. Then place the cross between the black heart and the white one and say that when Jesus died, He made a way for our hearts to be clean.

Jesus
Is Alive

When Jesus died, His friends
buried Him in a tomb.
They were so sad.

One day. Two days. Three days
    went by.
Then some of His friends went
    to the tomb again.

Surprise! An angel was there.
He was so bright and shiny
    that the friends were frightened.
The angel said, "Go tell Jesus' other
    friends that He is alive!"

They ran to find the other friends.
"Jesus is alive! Jesus is alive!" they said.
The other friends couldn't believe it
    was true.
But it was.

Soon two of Jesus' friends went
    walking home to another town.
Another man came to walk with them.
"Why are you so sad?" He asked.

The man was Jesus, but they didn't know it was Him.
They liked talking to Him.
"Come to our house for dinner," they said.
When He thanked God for the food, the friends saw that the man was Jesus!
He was alive!

PARENTS: The best news in the whole world is that Jesus is alive. As you read, have your little one make happy or sad faces to go with the story. Then talk with your child about a "forever smile" because Jesus is alive forever.

Luke 24:33–53;
Acts 1:6–11

Jesus Goes to Heaven

After Jesus came back to life, He visited His friends.
He would talk with them and teach them.
And then . . . He would disappear.
Jesus visited with His friends for many days.

But one day, it was time for Jesus to go to
  heaven.
It was time to say good-bye.
Jesus went with His friends to a hill.
A big cloud came down and covered Him up.

Then Jesus was lifted up into heaven.
Two angels came. They said, "Just as Jesus
     went away in the clouds, someday He will
     come back in the clouds."

We are still waiting for our
     Best Friend, Jesus, to come back.
He will come, and when He does,
     we will be with Him forever!

PARENTS: Help your little one imagine heaven. It is a wonderful place where no one is hurt or sad. The streets are made of gold, and there are homes for everyone. And best of all, Jesus and God are there.

Jesus Loves You

Jesus knows all about you.
He knows what color skin you have.
He knows what color eyes you have.
He knows if you are short or tall.
And He loves everything about you.

Jesus cares when you are hungry.
He cares when you get hurt.
He cares when you are sad and
    when you are happy.

Jesus sends His angels to protect
you and watch over you.
He loves you best of all.

PARENTS: Cut a heart shape from paper. Paste a picture
of Jesus on the heart and read the story again. Place the
picture near your little one's bed to comfort her.

The Father has loved us so much!
He loved us so much that we are
called children of God.
And we really are his children.

—1 John 3:1